Exploration and Encounters

Rosemary Rees
Sue Styles
Richard Scollins

HEINEMANN
EDUCATIONAL

CONTENTS

Heinemann Educational,
a division of Heinemann Educational Books Ltd,
Halley Court, Jordan Hill, Oxford OX2 8EJ

OXFORD LONDON EDINBURGH MADRID
ATHENS BOLOGNA PARIS MELBOURNE
SYDNEY AUCKLAND SINGAPORE TOKYO
IBADAN NAIROBI HARARE GABORONE
PORTSMOUTH NH(USA)

First published 1992

**British Library Cataloguing in Publication
Data** is available from the British Library on
request.

Designed by Ron Kamen, Green Door Design
Ltd, Basingstoke

Maps by Jeff Edwards, illustration on page 21 by
Dave Barnett

Printed in Spain by Mateu Cromo

Acknowledgements
The author and publisher would like to thank
the following for permission to reproduce
photographs:
Akademische Druk und Verlagsanstalt, Graz:
10A
Ancient Art and Architecture Collection: 4G
(Richard Stirling), 6B, 7G

Arxiu MAS: 8A, 9C, 9E, 11A
Biblioteca Laurenziano, Florence: 6E
Biblioteca Nazionale Centrale, Florence: 5C (M.
Schiopetto)
Bibliothèque Nationale/E. T. Archive: 2A
Bodleian Library, Oxford: 2D, 2E, 4E, 5E, 5F, 7A,
11B, 11C
British Library, London: 1E, 1I, 1J, 2B
Werner Forman Archive: 5D, 5G, 5H, 6A, 7B,
7C, 7E, 7F
Giraudon/Bridgeman Art Library: 4H, 9A
Michael Holford: 3E, 3F, 3G, 6D, 9F
Hubert Josse, Paris: 1G
Ander McIntyre: 4D
Museum für Völkerkunde, Vienna: 7D
Nasa/Science Photo Library: 1A
National Museums and Galleries on
Merseyside: 5B
G. Dagli Orti: 3A, 4A, 4F
Roger-Viollet: 8B, 8C
Royal Geographical Society: 10D
Scala: 9D

Cover illustration: Atlas by Diego Homen,
showing South America and Portugal c. 1558
(British Library/Bridgeman Art Library)

The illustrations on pages 23 (Source C) and 37
are reproduced from *See Through History: The
Aztecs*, Hamlyn Children's Books, 1992.

Every effort has been made to contact copyright
holders of material reproduced in this book.
Any omissions will be rectified in subsequent
printings if notice is given to the publisher.

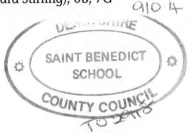

1 What did people know about the world 500 years ago?

Do you want to be an explorer? Do you want to cut your way through steamy jungles? Do you want to climb the highest mountains in the world? Do you want to tramp across frozen ice-fields? Perhaps you would sooner stay at home. If you want to, you can explore any country in the world. But wherever you go, someone else will have been there before you.

Men and women have made maps of every country and continent. They have measured coasts, rivers and mountains. They have drawn plans of cities, towns and villages. You will have to travel to the planets and the stars if you want to explore unknown places. It was not always like this.

Hundreds of years ago it was difficult to travel anywhere. It was dangerous, too. Merchants and sailors were often away for months and sometimes years. When they got back home they told everyone what they had seen and where they thought they had been. They drew maps and charts. Gradually people living in Europe put together a picture of what they thought the world was like.

Source A

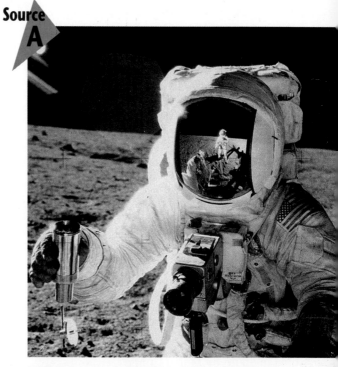

This is a photograph of an astronaut walking on the moon. It was taken in November 1969.

Source B

If there were no obstacles, a man could go round the earth as a fly crawls round an apple.

This was written in the 1200s.

Obstacle = Think about an obstacle race. You can't get easily to the end because there are things in the way stopping you from running straight and fast. An obstacle is something which gets in the way.

Source C

Brother Mauro, an Italian monk, drew this map of the world in 1459.

Many people thought that the world was flat and round – like a saucer. They said that if you travelled too far, you would fall over the edge and never be seen again. Other people, and most sailors, had worked out that the world was round – like a ball.

Ideas about the world

In 1490 ... some people thought that the world was flat BUT

... other people, and most sailors, thought that the world was round like a flattened ball.

... people in Europe did not know that America existed BUT

... the Europeans were starting to explore the world.

Merchants, sailors and travellers told tales about the wonderful things they had seen and the strange people they had met.

Source D

We saw on the shore a huge giant who danced, leaped and sang, while throwing sand and dust over his head. He had a large face, painted round with red; his eyes were ringed with yellow and in the middle of his cheeks were painted two hearts. He had hardly any hair on his head, what little he had being painted white.

Antonio Pigafetta wrote this. He went round the world with the explorer Magellan between 1519 and 1522.

Source F

There is another isle where people have one foot, and that foot is so broad it covers all the body and shades it from the Sun. On this foot they run so fast it is a wonder to see.

From a book written by Sir John Mandeville in about 1360. He said he had travelled around the world for 35 years, but a lot of his book was copied from earlier books.

Source E

This was drawn by Hartman Schedel in 1493.

This painting shows Europeans arriving in far distant lands. It was painted in about 1400.

Source H

In the harbour there are some very white and beautiful people, who wear boots and hats of iron and never stay in any place. They eat a sort of white stone and drink blood.

A man living in Sri Lanka wrote this in the 16th century about some visitors to his country.

Explorers before Columbus

1275–95   Marco Polo, a Venetian merchant, travels overland to China. He first went to China with his uncle and his father. He is the most well-known of the three though, because he wrote a book about the journey.

1415–75   Portuguese sailors find the Canary Islands and explore the coast of West Africa.

1486–87   Bartholomew Diaz sails round the southern tip of Africa.

Olaus Magnus drew this map in 1572.

Most people in the 1500s were frightened of travelling to unknown lands. This was not only because they thought they might meet monsters. People were also frightened of the ordinary dangers of sea travel, and of travelling without maps.

A lot of people were frightened by the stories told by merchants and sailors. Many men and women believed that if you sailed north you would go into a world of darkness. The seas would turn solid and your blood would freeze. If you travelled south the seas would boil and your skin would be burned black. If you travelled east, overland into Asia, you might be attacked by natives or eaten by wild animals. If you travelled west, into the great **Ocean Sea** (the Atlantic Ocean), you would make the most frightening journey it was possible to make. You would sail into seas full of huge monsters, and would probably never be seen again.

People were frightened about things they did not know or understand. They were frightened, too, of things which they knew really happened. People knew that terrible storms wrecked ships and drowned sailors. They knew that sailors caught all kinds of diseases and often died on long voyages. Only very brave people dared to travel into the unknown.

Source J

Some people believed that sea monsters wrecked ships and drowned sailors.

How do we know?

We know what people thought the world was like by looking at the things they wrote or drew. This unit has used pictures, written sources and maps from several different countries to try to give an idea of what Europeans knew about the world.

The sources tell you different things. Some of these are shown in the table.

Sentence	Source
People knew more about Europe than about Africa and India.	Source C
People thought that there were strange-looking people in far distant lands.	Sources E, G, D and F
People believed in sea monsters which attacked ships.	Sources I, J

We cannot say that all Europeans believed these things, just some of them. There is no way we can tell what everyone thought.

2 Why did Columbus sail west? What did he find there?

When you next go to your local shop or supermarket look for the shelf where the spices are kept. Five or six hundred years ago these spices cost a lot of money. So did goods like silk and silver, diamonds and ivory. Only rich people could afford to buy them.

Merchants and traders brought goods into Europe from China, India and the Spice Islands. Europeans called this part of the world 'the Indies'. Some merchants travelled overland between Europe and the Indies. They travelled across hot deserts and over rocky mountains. Some sent their goods by ships. All journeys were difficult and sometimes dangerous. They took a very long time.

Source A

A picture painted during the 1400s. It shows people gathering peppers to sell to a European merchant.

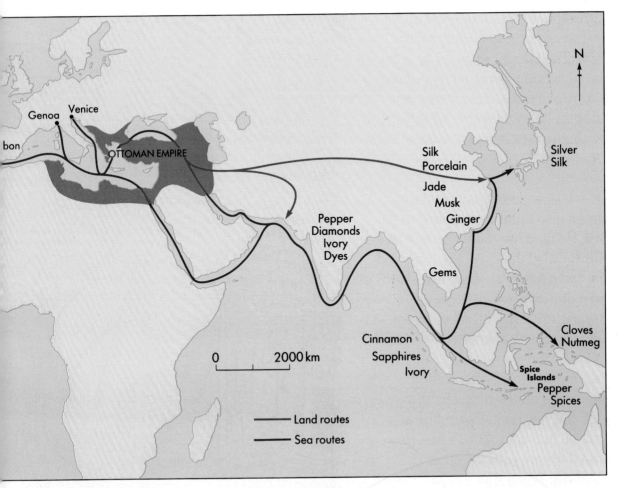

Map labels:
- N (compass)
- Genoa
- Venice
- bon
- OTTOMAN EMPIRE
- Silk / Porcelain
- Silver / Silk
- Jade
- Musk
- Ginger
- Pepper / Diamonds / Ivory / Dyes
- Gems
- Cloves / Nutmeg
- Cinnamon / Sapphires / Ivory
- Spice Islands
- Pepper / Spices
- 0   2000 km
- —— Land routes
- —— Sea routes

This modern map shows what merchants and traders bought in the Indies, and the routes they took to get there and back again to Europe.

All the trade routes to Europe from the Indies went through lands called the **Ottoman Empire**. The rulers of the Ottoman Empire made the traders and merchants pay large taxes on the goods they were carrying. The merchants had to charge extra high prices for their goods when they got back to Europe. Soon even very rich people would not be able to buy goods from the Indies. Someone had to find a new route to the East.

Trade routes

Rich people in Europe wanted spices, silks and jewels. These had to be brought from far-away countries like China and the Indies.

Traders brought these goods overland from the east to Europe. This took a long time and was also dangerous. The spices, silks and jewels were valuable and this made the traders targets for robbers. No one had yet sailed westwards over the Ocean Sea from Europe to find the Indies.

Christopher Columbus grew up in the busy port of Genoa, Italy. He learned to sail ships, to steer by the stars and to work out speed and distance at sea. Columbus worked out that he could reach the Indies by sailing west across the great Ocean Sea.

Queen Isabella of Spain said she would give Columbus money to do this. He used her money to hire three ships, called the *Pinta*, the *Nina* and the *Santa Maria*. He also hired 90 men and boys to sail them. In August 1492 they all set out from Spain, into the unknown.

Two months later, after sailing westwards all the time, the ship's look-out saw land. Columbus was sure he had got to the Indies. He rowed ashore with the other captains. When they landed they all thanked God, kissed the sand, and set up the royal banner of Spain.

The people who lived there told Columbus he had landed on an island called **Guanahani**. They were Arawak people. Columbus called them 'Indians' because he was sure he had found the Indies. He called the island San Salvador.

In January 1493 Columbus sailed back to Europe. He took with him gold and jewels, birds, plants and even some Indians. They came from the islands he had explored.

Source B

This woodcut shows Columbus sailing by some of the islands near San Salvador.

Source C

Half an hour before sunrise, I set my course for the Canary Islands, which are in the Ocean Sea, from there to set off on a voyage that will last until I arrive in the Indies.

Columbus kept a journal. In it he wrote down what happened each day. This is part of what he wrote on 3 August 1492.

This picture shows Columbus landing on the island he called San Salvador. It was drawn in 1594.

Most people thought Columbus had found a way to the Indies by sailing west. Some people were puzzled. They thought that Columbus had not sailed far enough to have reached the Indies. He hadn't brought any silks or spices back with him, either. Just where had he been?

Columbus

Christopher Columbus was Italian, but Queen Isabella of Spain gave him money for his voyage across the Ocean Sea.

In 1492 Columbus landed on the island of San Salvador. This is an island off the coast of North America. Columbus thought he had landed in Japan or China. He called it San Salvador – Saint of Salvation – to give thanks to God.

It took Columbus 36 days to cross the Ocean Sea. A ship today can cross to America in four days. If you fly to America in Concorde it will take just under three hours.

A modern map showing Columbus's four voyages.

1st voyage (1492)
2nd voyage (1493–6)
3rd voyage (1498)
4th voyage (1502–4)

NORTH AMERICA

ATLANTIC OCEAN

PORTUGAL SPAIN
Lisbon
Seville
Cadiz

Canary Islands

Cuba

Hispaniola

AFRICA

Azores

Trinidad

SOUTH AMERICA

Christopher Columbus crossed the Ocean Sea three more times. On the map you can see the different routes he sailed and the places he explored. Each voyage made Columbus more sure than ever that he had reached the Indies. He thought that islands like Cuba, Hispaniola and Trinidad were just off the coast of China. He was wrong.

Columbus's fourth voyage ended in 1504. He never went to sea again. Queen Isabella was dying. Her husband, King Ferdinand, was not interested in Columbus. He knew that Columbus had not found a way to the Indies by sailing west across the Ocean Sea. He thought that Columbus had failed. Columbus died two years later. He never knew that he had been exploring a whole world which hardly anyone in Europe had guessed was there.

Soon, men like Robert Thorne were drawing maps which were very different from the one drawn by Brother Mauro in 1459 (see page 5).

This map was drawn by an Englishman,
Robert Thorne, in 1527.

What do people say about the past?

People who write about the past do not always agree. Sometimes the evidence is not clear, and people say different things.

Most people think that Christopher Columbus discovered America. But there is evidence to show that the Vikings were there before him. So who 'discovered' America? Look at some arguments for and against, below.

'1492 Christopher Columbus sailed over the Atlantic Ocean. He was the first person to discover America. He was one of the greatest explorers who ever lived.'

Hank

Ilsa

'In 1000 AD the Vikings landed in North America.'

For	Against
The Vikings discovered America. They were there first.	No one but the Vikings really knew it was there.
Columbus discovered America. He was the one who told people about it.	There is clear evidence that the Vikings were there first, not Columbus.

3 What was life like on board ship 500 years ago?

This painting
of caravels was
made in the 1500s.

Caravels were the best ships for making ocean voyages. They were small, fast and easy to steer. Two of Christopher Columbus's first ships, the *Pinta* and the *Nina*, were caravels. Life for the sailors on a caravel was tough. It was also dangerous. There were violent storms. Ships were often wrecked. Every day began with prayers. The sailors prayed that they would be kept safe from harm.

Caravels were about 21 metres long and 6.5 metres wide. Below decks the crew had to store all the food and drink they would need on the voyage. They also had to store the sails, ropes and firewood. There had to be room for the **tiller** and the **anchor**. There had to be room, too, for any treasure they might bring back.

Sailors lived and slept on the open deck, no matter what the weather was like. They usually had one hot meal a day, which was cooked on deck. They ate the fresh food at the start of the voyage, before it went bad. Then they ate hard ship's biscuit, salted meat and fish. Rats and maggots usually got to the food, while it was stored in the hold. The sailors drank water or water mixed with wine. The water was stored in wooden barrels. After a week or two it tasted bad. The wine sometimes turned into vinegar.

Sailors got terrible diseases and many of them died. In hot parts of the world they were sometimes ill with **malaria** and **yellow fever**. The disease they got most often was **scurvy**. This was because they could not eat fresh fruit or vegetables on long voyages. No one knew, then, why sailors got scurvy. They only knew that it was a dreadful illness.

Source B

We ate only old biscuit reduced to powder, all full of worms and stinking of the urine that the rats made on it. And we drank water that was yellow and stinking.

Antonio Pigafetta wrote this in the 1500s. He sailed across the Pacific Ocean with Magellan. He is telling what they ate when they had been at sea for nearly four months.

Source C

It rotted all my gums, which gave out a black and putrid blood. My thighs and lower legs were black, and I was forced to use my knife each day to cut into the flesh, to release this black and foul blood.

A 15th-century sailor describes what it was like to have scurvy.

Life on board ship was still very hard ...

... fresh food went bad quickly
... rats and maggots got at the rest of the food.
... sailors had to sleep on deck or wherever there was room
... sailors caught terrible diseases.

This is a modern photograph of a sand-glass which is about 500 years old.

The crew of about 30 sailors was divided into two groups. Each group was called a **watch**. A watch worked for four hours and then rested for four hours. While one watch rested, the other watch worked. Time was measured by a **half-hour sand glass**. It was the job of the ship's boy to turn the glass over as the sand ran out. He had to shout out the time, too.

All wooden ships leak. The first job of each watch was to pump the sea water out. If there were any gaps between the wooden planks, the crew filled them with rope and sealed them with hot tar. They scrubbed the decks and pulled on heavy ropes to move the sails. Sometimes, when the weather was very bad, they had to pull the sails down; when the weather was better and the wind blowing in the right direction, they put the sails up again. The watch checked the cargo. They mended sails and ropes. Some sailors were look-outs. They climbed to the **crow's nest** at the top of the mast. Their job was to shout out if they saw land, or another ship, or any kind of danger.

Sailors worked for a four-hour watch and then rested for four hours.

Time was measured by a half-hour sand-glass.

◄ Life on board ship was hard and dangerous 500 years ago.

In the 1500s it was very difficult to take a ship from place to place if the captain could not see land. Sailors made charts of the sea routes to all the places they most often visited. But ships sailing into unknown seas had no charts to help them. How did they manage?

All ships had a **compass**. This told the captain whether his **helmsman** was steering north, south, east or west. Many sailors used a **quadrant**. This told the sailors how far north of the equator they were.

Source
G

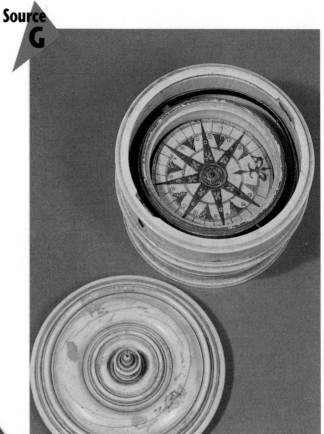

This is a photograph of a compass used in the 1500s.

Source
F

This is a photograph of a traverse board used in the 1500s. Details about the direction a ship was sailing, and the distance it had travelled, were pegged out on a traverse board. The traverse board was always propped up in front of the helmsman.

Sailors needed to work out how fast their ship was travelling. They dropped a piece of wood over the side. They used a sand-glass to measure the time it took for the ship to pass the wood. On some ships a long piece of rope was tied to a log of wood. **Knots** were tied in the rope. A sailor threw the wood over the side. He timed the speed at which the knots ran through his hands. This way he knew how fast the ship was sailing and could work out how far it had sailed.

This modern drawing shows the helmsman's table. Can you see the compass, sand-glass, and traverse board? The helmsman used all these to steer the ship. He obeyed his captain's orders. The captain checked the compass and traverse board. He checked the readings made from the quadrant. Then he decided what course the helmsman had to steer. He kept a careful note of everything in his **log book**. He would be blamed if anything went wrong.

Navigation was a very skilled job. Sailors used each of these instruments: compass, quadrant, sand-glass, traverse board.

Some of these were difficult to use.

Were things different then?

Caravels were about 21 metres long by 6.5 metres wide. One of the modern ships which sails from England to France is 179 metres long and 25.36 metres wide.

Caravels depended on the weather. They could not sail in the direction of the wind was coming from. A modern ship can sail in any direction. Columbus's crew slept anywhere. Today crew members have cabins of their own.

4 Who were the Aztecs?

The islands Christopher Columbus explored were not empty lands. People lived there. It was the same on the mainland of America. Look back to the map on page 14. Can you find Columbus's 4th voyage? He sailed along the coast of Central America. There were many different groups of people living there. Some were hunters and some were farmers. Some lived in towns, and some wandered from place to place. The **Aztecs** were one of the strongest and most powerful groups. Columbus did not know this. Neither did the Europeans who followed him to America.

The Aztec people had not always been strong and powerful. For hundreds of years they had wandered from place to place. They were looking for somewhere to settle. In about the year 1300 they came to the Valley of **Mexico** and **Lake Texcoco**. They moved on to swampy islands in the middle of the lake. The Aztecs fished and farmed. They built houses from sticks and reeds covered with mud. They built a temple for one of their gods, **Huitzilopochtli.** They were on Lake Texcoco to stay; they were not going to move on.

Source A

This Aztec picture shows Aztec chiefs setting out on their journey to find a new land.

The Aztec god, Huitzilopochtli, told the Aztec chiefs that they had to travel south. There they would build a large city on a swamp. Huitzilopochtli said that the Aztecs would know when they had come to the right place. This was because they would see an eagle sitting on a cactus. The eagle would be eating a snake. As soon as the Aztecs saw the eagle, the cactus and the snake, they were to stop their wanderings and build a city. The Aztecs wandered until they came to Lake Texcoco. There they were chased onto an island by an angry ruler. On the island they saw, in a cave, the eagle, the cactus and the snake. They knew they had to build a city and settle down.

This is the Aztecs' story about the way they came to live on an island in the middle of Lake Texcoco.

This is a modern drawing of the Aztec god Huitzilopochtli.

Thousands of years ago Asia and North America were joined together. So much water was frozen in the ice-caps and glaciers that the sea was lower. People from Asia wandered over to North America, following the animals which they needed for food.

When the Ice Age ended the level of the seas rose and the land-bridge was flooded.

This is the modern badge of Mexico.

The Aztecs fought and fought until they captured all the lands, towns and villages for hundreds of miles around Lake Texcoco. The Aztecs forced the rulers of the towns they had defeated to send **tribute** to them. They drew up detailed lists showing exactly what goods each town had to pay to the Aztec state. These goods might be animal skins, black beans, blankets, red peppers, jade beads or shields. The defeated people became poor. They hated the Aztecs. They were also terrified of them. The Aztecs became very rich and very powerful. They called their lands **Anahuac**.

The Aztecs built a beautiful city on their island in the middle of Lake Texcoco. They turned the whole island into a city, which they called **Tenochtitlan**. They used mud to make the island bigger and they dug canals to connect up different parts of their island city. They built an enormous **aqueduct** to bring fresh water to the city. They built huge **causeways** to join Tenochtitlan to the mainland.

The Aztecs built big stone temples and beautiful palaces, houses for ordinary people, a zoo and gardens full of brightly-coloured flowers. By 1502 about 300,000 people lived and worked in Tenochtitlan. It was bigger than any city in Europe at that time.

This is an Aztec tribute sheet. It shows what some towns had to pay the Aztecs. The towns are drawn in the left-hand column. By the side of each town are pictures of the things which the Aztecs wanted.

This plan of Tenochtitlan was printed in Germany in 1523.
It was copied from a sketch made by a European, Hernan
Cortes, who visited Tenochtitlan a few years earlier.

The Aztecs and Tenochtitlan

The Aztecs were once poor and weak.
Later, they became the most powerful
tribe in the area. They made other
tribes pay tribute to them. The Aztecs
and the other tribes did not use
money. The tribes gave the Aztecs
goods like food, jewels and weapons.

The Aztecs built a beautiful city on an
island in the middle of Lake Texcoco.
The city was called Tenochtitlan.
The name Tenochtitlan means 'the
place of the prickly pear cactus'.

Tenochtitlan was bigger than any city
in Europe at the time.

The Aztec emperor was chosen by the noble families. The person they chose had to be a nobleman. He had to be a trained priest and a good fighter. In 1502 the noble families chose **Montezuma** to be their emperor.

The Aztecs treated Montezuma as if he was a god. He wore the finest clothes. His sandals had soles made from pure gold. When he travelled outside his palace he was carried on a richly decorated throne by four nobles. No one was allowed to look directly at his face.

Montezuma had a huge palace. Hundreds of people lived and worked there. At mealtimes his servants had to cook more than 1,000 plates of food. Montezuma ate the very best food. Sometimes his advisors stood by his table and talked to him while he ate. They were not allowed to look at him. If he offered them food, they had to eat it standing up. Montezuma drank chocolate after a meal. No one in Europe had ever seen chocolate.

While Montezuma was emperor, the Aztec empire grew bigger than ever before. Montezuma was very rich and very powerful.

Source
G

This is a modern photograph of the great feather headdress which Montezuma wore in processions.

Source
H

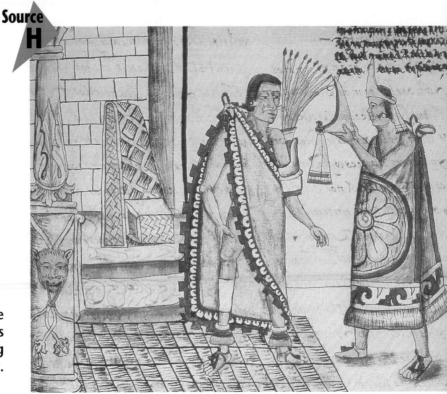

This picture, made in 1502, shows Montezuma being crowned emperor.

How did things change?

Historians look at things in the past which changed and things which stayed the same. Both these things are important, not just the changes.

One reason for studying things that change and things that stay the same is to find out what was important to people.

Between 1300 and 1500 some things changed for the Aztecs. Other things stayed the same. Below are some things which changed, and some which stayed the same. In the box are some changes, and the effects that they had.

Things that changed

They fought other tribes.
They became powerful.
They built a city, Tenochtitlan.

Things which stayed the same

They spoke the same language.
They believed in the same gods.

Change	Effect
They fought other tribes.	They became powerful and rich.
They built a permanent home.	They had a base to build an empire.

5 What was life like in the Aztec Empire?

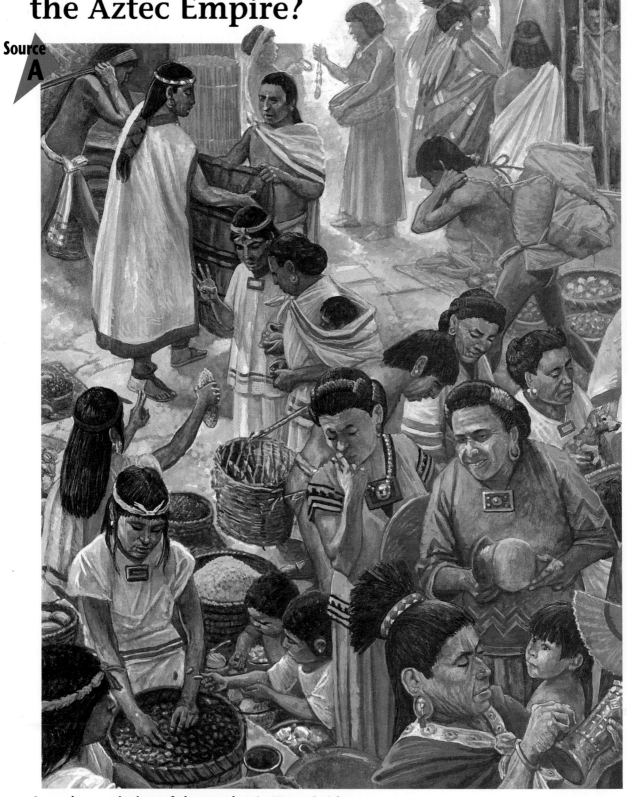

A modern painting of the market in Tenochtitlan.

Every day a great market was held in the centre of Tenochtitlan. Merchants and traders, farmers and craftworkers brought goods to the market from all over the Aztec empire. They brought luxuries like jade necklaces, silver bracelets and golden drinking beakers. They brought ordinary things like black beans, flour, rabbits, puppies, pottery dishes and tobacco pipes. They brought slaves and put them in cages for people to look at and buy. Every day more than 60,000 people went to the market.

The Aztecs did not use money. They took their goods to market to swap them for what they wanted. If two Aztecs couldn't make an exact swap, one of them would add in a few cocoa beans. As a rough guide to the number of beans needed, Aztecs agreed that 100 cocoa beans were worth 1 cloak; a slave was worth 25 cloaks, and a jade necklace was worth 600 cloaks.

Look at the people in the picture opposite. The Aztecs had very strict rules about clothes. Nobles were allowed to wear brightly-coloured cloaks and richly patterned loin-cloths. Ordinary people had to make their clothes from plain, undyed cloth. The Aztecs had strict rules about hairstyles, too. Girls could have their hair loose; as soon as a girl married she had to plait her hair and wind the plaits around her head. Warriors tied their hair in a topknot. They were allowed to wear jewels in their lips, ears and noses at special times.

This is an Aztec picture of a merchant. Some merchants worked for the government. They brought back information about plots and rebellions in far-away towns. They brought back information about strangers who had arrived in the Aztec empire.

The Aztecs did not use money. When they went to market they swapped goods, including slaves.

Some merchants were spies for the Aztec emperor. He needed their information about strangers in the Aztec empire.

Poor Aztecs lived in one roomed houses on the edge of Tenochtitlan. The walls of their houses were made from **wattle and daub**. Richer people, like craftworkers, lived closer to the middle of Tenochtitlan. Their houses were built with mud-bricks and had rooms which led on to a central courtyard. Nobles lived in palaces in the middle of Tenochtitlan which were built from stone. Most of the palaces had over 100 rooms and courtyards and patios which were full of flowers. The stone walls were decorated with carvings.

This is an Aztec picture of a bath-house. Most rich Aztecs built one in their garden. They lit fires around the outside until the walls were red hot. Then they went inside and splashed water on the walls to make steam. In the steam they beat themselves with twigs until their skin was clean.

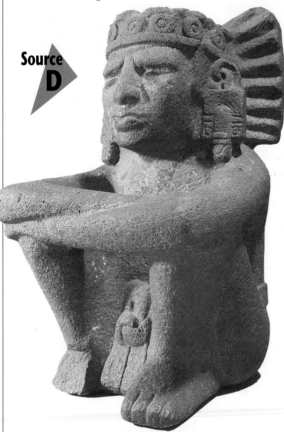

This is a carved statue of the god Xiuhtectuhtli. Aztecs used to put statues like this by the fireplace in their homes. They called them household gods.

Aztecs did not have much furniture. Everyone slept on mats on the floor. They sat on cushions filled with straw. The most important part of all Aztec houses was the fireplace. This was where the cooking was done. Aztecs ate **tortillas**, which were a sort of pancake made from maize flour. They ate a lot of vegetables, fish and frogs, tadpoles and newts. On special occasions they might roast a duck, a rabbit, a chicken or a puppy. Rich people often ate pheasant and wild pig. Everyone ate with their fingers.

Aztec parents were very strict with their children. They taught them at home. The children learned the sorts of things they would need to do when they were grown-up. Boys were taught fishing and woodwork; girls were taught cooking and weaving. Every boy had to go to school when he was eight. Some boys went to schools where they learned how to be priests. Other boys went to schools where they learned how to be warriors. Girls did not have to go to school. Girls could learn to be priestesses and healers if they went to school.

This Aztec picture shows fathers teaching their sons, and mothers teaching their daughters.

Tenochtitlan was carefully planned and built. The builders were skillful. For example, the outsides of rich people's houses were plastered with a kind of cement which made them white and shiny. This kept the houses cool because the white plaster reflected the hot rays of the sun.

Aztec children were punished by their parents when they were naughty. Sometimes they were pricked with thorns.

Aztecs did not use letters to make words when they wrote. Instead they drew tiny pictures called **glyphs** to show what they wanted to say. There were very strict rules which all writers had to follow. Each picture was always drawn in the same way, so everyone knew what the writer meant.

Aztecs who were very good at reading and writing could become **scribes**. They could then do important work for the government. They could write down the empire's laws or write out the tribute sheets. All priests could read and write well. They had to write religious books and history books. Aztec books are called **codices**. They were made out of bark paper or deer-skin. The pages were joined together in a long zig-zag.

These are some of the glyphs used by the Aztecs.

The Aztecs stuck pieces of paper together to make a long book called a codex.

Aztec nobles played a game called **tlachtli** at special times like religious festivals. Two teams played on a stone court surrounded by stone walls. To score, one team had to get a small bouncing rubber ball into the other team's end of the court. The game would be won at once if one side managed to get the ball through their opponent's stone ring, which was fixed high on a wall. The players were only allowed to touch the ball with their knees, elbows or hips. The game was fierce and fast. Players were often hurt and sometimes killed. Everyone came to watch and cheer on their team.

All Aztecs played a game called **patolli**. They had to throw dice and move coloured beans on a board until they got three beans in a row. Many Aztecs lost all they had playing patolli. They and their families had to become slaves.

Were things different then?

Not all Aztecs lived the same sort of lives.

- Boys and girls were taught different skills and tasks.
- Aztec nobles played tlachtli.
- All Aztecs played patolli.
- Poor Aztecs lived in small houses made from branches and clay.
- Rich Aztecs lived in houses made of stone.
- All Aztecs slept on mats on the floor.
- Poor Aztecs ate food which they could catch or grow, like vegetables, frogs and newts.
- Rich Aztecs often ate pheasant and wild pig.
- All Aztecs ate with their fingers.

Source 1

This Aztec picture shows people playing patolli.

6 What did the Aztecs believe?

The Aztecs believed in many gods and goddesses. Each one looked after a different part of Aztec life. Three gods were more important than all the others. **Huitzilopochtli** was the god of sun and war. **Tezcatlipoca** was the god of night and evil. **Quetzalcoatl** was the god of life. Aztecs believed that one day Quetzalcoatl would come to earth to decide what was to happen to all the Aztec people.

The Aztecs believed their gods watched them all the time. They were afraid of doing something to make their gods angry. They built huge stone **pyramids**. At the top of each one they built a **temple** for religious **ceremonies** and **sacrifices**. Aztecs believed their gods wanted human blood. Aztec priests sacrificed thousands of men, women and children in the temples. In wars the Aztecs captured people for sacrifice. Aztecs thought that if they did not give human hearts and blood to the gods, then the gods would destroy the world.

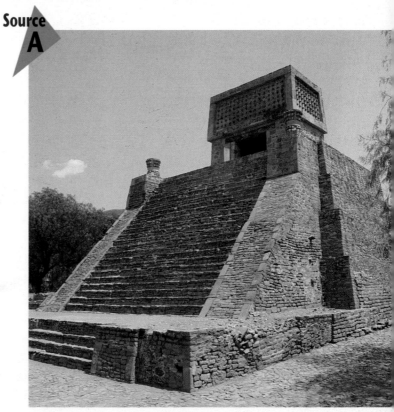

Source A

This is a photograph of a modern copy of an Aztec temple.

Source B

This Aztec knife was used in temple sacrifices.

R S COLLINS

A modern painting of an Aztec sacrifice.

Priests were very powerful people. The emperor did not go to war until he had asked their advice. People asked a priest before they went on a journey or named a baby. Aztecs believed that some days were lucky and some unlucky. It would be terrible to do something important on an unlucky day.

Only the priests could tell them which days were lucky and unlucky. This was because only the priests understood the **sacred calendar**. A baby born on day *4 Dog*, for example, would do well; one born on *2 Rabbit* would become a drunk. A good day for painters was *7 Flower*, and merchants always had to travel on *1 Ocelot*. Priests used the sacred calendar to tell the future too – whether there was going to be a flood, or an earthquake or an invasion. Priestesses worked with the priests. They could do everything the priests did, except make sacrifices.

As well as the sacred calendar, the Aztecs had a sun calendar which they called **haab**. This divided the year into 365 days. Every 52 years the first day of the sacred calendar and the first day of the sun calendar were on the same day. The Aztecs were afraid that on this day the world would end.

Source D

An Aztec statue of Coatlicue, their Earth goddess.

Source E

An Aztec picture showing a man in year 52. He is getting ready for the end of the world by throwing away all his goods.

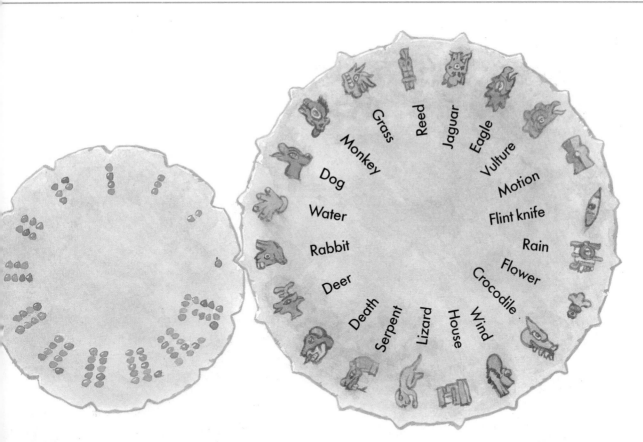

This shows you how the sacred calendar works. The calendar is made up of two wheels. The small wheel on the left has thirteen numbers painted on it. The large wheel on the right has the names of twenty days painted on it. The small wheel turns clockwise. The large wheel turns anti-clockwise. Each number then fits with a day.

Why did things happen?

Why did the Aztecs sacrifice humans to their gods?

They believed that their gods were very powerful.

If they gave human hearts and blood to their gods, this would help to keep them strong and powerful. If they did not do this, they thought that the world would come to an end.

7 Aztec craft and technology: what did they make?

This Aztec picture shows fathers teaching their sons special craft skills.

Aztecs did not use money. People were thought to be rich if they owned beautiful things. So an Aztec who owned two bowls with gold and black decorations painted on them was richer than one who had ten ordinary pottery bowls. Rich Aztecs employed the very best **craftworkers** to make the things they needed. Craftworkers were very important people in the Aztec empire.

Different groups of people living in the Aztec empire were better at some crafts than others. The **Mixtecs**, for example, were skilled goldworkers. The people of **Cholula** made the very best pottery. All craftworkers were respected by the other Aztecs. Craftworkers lived and worked in their own separate areas of Aztec cities. They worshipped their own gods. Usually whole families worked at the same craft. Parents taught their children the special skills they needed.

The Aztecs built palaces and temples from stone. Look back at page 34 and you will see one of the temples. Aztec stoneworkers made beautiful and complicated carvings too. They made carvings of their gods (look at page 36). They made carvings of dragons, strange beasts and patterns to decorate their temples and palaces. They made carvings about their history and the way they thought the Aztec world would end.

The Aztecs did not have wheels, so they could not use carts or pulleys to carry and lift the stone they used in building. Slaves carried everything. Aztecs did not have iron from which to make knives and chisels to cut and carve their stone. They used blades made from a mixture of copper and tin or from polished **obsidian**.

Source B

The great Calendar Stone, which told how the Aztec world would end. It was once painted in bright colours.

Information box

The Aztecs knew about the wheel. They used it for children's toys. They did not use it to make carts or wagons. They also did not have any horses.

They did not make pottery on a potter's wheel. They made pottery from coils of clay, piled one on top of another.

The Aztecs had plenty of gold, silver, copper and tin. They did not have iron.

Aztecs made their clothes from fibre which they got from a cactus plant. Richard Aztecs sometimes had clothes made from cotton. All clothes were very brightly coloured.

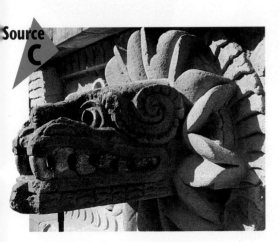

Source C

A carving on the temple of Quetzalcoatl at Teotihuacan.

Aztecs were experts at working with feathers. They used feathers to make huge shields and headdresses which were worn by Aztec kings, nobles and warriors at special times. Look back at page 26 and you will see the headdress which Montezuma wore. Aztecs also used feathers to decorate the clothes of rich people. Sometimes the featherworkers used so many feathers that a whole cloak or skirt looked as if it was made out of feathers and nothing else. Featherworkers made complete outfits for warriors to wear in battle. Some workers made pictures out of feathers. The very best feathers to use were the ones from the green **quetzal** bird and those from the blue **hummingbird**.

Source D

This feather shield belonged to an Aztec king.

Source E

Aztec potters made beautifully shaped bowls, dishes, jugs and drinking cups. They usually painted richly coloured patterns and pictures on the outsides of the pots.

Aztecs did not use wheels at all. They did not use potters' wheels. They made coil pots. When a pot was the right shape, the potter smoothed the outside until there were no bumps left.

Goldsmiths made delicate gold ornaments. They made gold earrings, necklaces, **nose plugs** and **lip plugs** for nobles and important warriors. They made all kinds of wonderful objects for priests, kings and emperors.

Aztecs worked with precious stones like **rubies**. They used **jade** and **turquoise** to make beautiful masks, ornaments and jewellery.

Source F

This snake was made from wood and then covered in turquoise. It was part of an Aztec headdress.

Source G

This gold ornament was made by the Mixtec people.

How do we know?

We can find out about Aztec craft and technology from different types of sources.

- From the temples and buildings in Mexico which are still standing today. We still have some of the pottery, the jewels and the weapons made by the Aztecs (like Sources D, E and F on pages 40 and 41).
- From the carvings which we can still see (like Sources B and C on page 39)
- We still have some of the Aztec books which the Spanish took back to Europe with them. (Source A on page 38 is from one of these)
- From descriptions of Aztec life written by some of Cortes' soldiers.

These sources show us that the Aztecs were ...

... skilled woodcarvers
... good at stone-carving
... skilled gold-workers
... expert at working with feathers
... skilled at making pots

8 How did Cortes and his men conquer the Aztec Empire?

Hernan Cortes was ten years old when news reached his town in Spain that Christopher Columbus had crossed the great Ocean Sea. As Cortes grew up he heard stories of a great empire in the West, full of gold and jewels. He longed to go there. He went first to Cuba. There he worked hard and became rich and important. He owned farms and mines. He wanted more than anything to rule a land of his own. Then the governor of Cuba asked him to lead an expedition to the mainland. This was Cortes's great chance.

In 1519 Cortes sailed for Mexico. He took with him 11 ships and 100 sailors, 508 soldiers, 16 horses, a few cannons and some muskets. They all landed safely on a part of Mexico which had not been explored before. Cortes burnt all the ships which had brought them there. There was no going back.

Source A

A painting of Cortes and his men in Mexico. It was painted in 1698.

guzmā.   michvacā.

This Aztec picture shows Cortes fighting.

Then Cortes ordered some of his men to stay behind. Cortes and 400 Spaniards began their long march to Tenochtitlan. They marched through steamy hot jungles. They marched over high mountains where the winds were icy. They fought off attacks by thousands of fierce Indian warriors. Cortes and his men always won. They used **muskets**, which the Indians had never seen before. They rode horses, which the Indians had never seen before. The Indians were amazed. They began to believe that Cortes was a god. Different Indian tribes agreed to fight with Cortes against the Aztecs, whom they hated and feared. (Look back at page 24 to remind yourself why.) Meanwhile, in Tenochtitlan, Montezuma listened to what his spies told him. He watched and waited.

New Spain

- Soon after they landed in Mexico Cortes and his men built a town. Cortes called it *Villa Rica de la Vera Cruz*. This means 'the rich town of the true cross'. The town had lots of big buildings. When it was finished it looked like a Spanish town.

- Cortes fought many Indians. He brought the Spanish way of fighting to the New World. Cortes and his men had muskets and cross-bows, lances and swords. Some rode on horses. The Indians had bows and arrows and spears. Cortes won every battle.

This Aztec picture shows Montezuma and some nobles giving presents to Cortes. A woman called Marina is standing behind Cortes. She was very useful to him because she could speak Spanish and Nahuatl, the Aztec language.

Montezuma was worried. No one had been able to stop these strange foreigners from marching further and further into the Aztec empire. Were they from from a hostile tribe across the sea, or were they something worse? It was a special year in the Aztec calendar. The Aztec priests said the god Quetzalcoatl would come back to destroy Tenochtitlan and the Aztec people. Montezuma decided that Cortes and his men were gods. He did not dare fight them, even though they seemed to be threatening his empire. Instead he welcomed them into Tenochtitlan.

Everything seemed to be going well for Cortes. However, he wanted to make sure that his men were safe in Tenochtitlan. There were, after all, only 400 of them and there were about 300,000 Aztecs. The Spaniards were staying in an Aztec palace. Cortes asked Montezuma to come and stay with them. Montezuma, the great Aztec emperor, was really Cortes's prisoner. He did everything Cortes asked him to. Then Cortes began to complain about the ways the Aztecs worshipped. He hated their gory human sacrifices. Montezuma was very angry.

Things went from bad to worse. A Spanish commander panicked because he heard tales of plots against Cortes. He ordered his men to kill hundreds of Aztecs as they danced at a religious festival. The Aztecs fought back. A fierce and bloody battle began.

'Our Lord, you are weary. The journey has tired you, but you have arrived on earth. You have come here to sit on your throne.'

This is what Montezuma said when he met Cortes. We know this because a young man called Bernal Diaz travelled with Cortes. When Diaz was 70 years old he wrote down everything he could remember.

We admired the high towers, pyramids and other buildings, all made of stone, which rose from the water. It was all so wonderful that I do not know how to describe this first glimpse of things never heard of, seen or dreamed of before.

Bernal Diaz, who travelled with Cortes, wrote this description of Tenochtitlan many years later.

Once upon a time the Aztec god Quetzalcoatl became angry with the Aztecs. He wanted to stop them sacrificing people to him. He was the god of wind and life. He loved and cared for people. He appeared in human form and asked them to stop killing people. The Indians would not listen to him. So he sailed away towards the sunrise. He said that he would return. He was tall, with a white skin, long, dark hair and a flowing beard. Cortes looked very like this.

Cortes and his men managed to fight their way out of Tenochtitlan, over the huge causeways. About 300 of them survived. They then had to face a vast Aztec army at a place called **Otumba**. The Aztecs tried to capture the Spaniards alive for sacrifice. The Spaniards concentrated on killing the Aztec commanders so that there would be no one to give orders to the warriors. Cortes and his men won.

Other Indian tribes quickly joined sides with Cortes. They wanted to help wipe out the hated Aztecs. They marched back to Tenochtitlan and fought their way into the city. They destroyed everything as they went. The Aztecs fought fiercely to defend their city, but it was hopeless. On 13th August 1521 the last Aztecs were massacred. Montezuma was dead. Tenochtitlan was a smoking ruin. The Aztec empire was gone for ever.

◄ A modern painting showing Cortes and his men fighting the Aztecs.

Look very carefully at Source F.

The artist who painted this picture was not there while the battle was going on. He is a modern artist who specializes in painting historial pictures. Where do you think he got his ideas from?

Look through the book and find some of the sources he might have used.

Why did things happen?

Cortes defeated the Aztecs for a number of reasons.

- Cortes wanted to be rich and famous. So he was determined to conquer the Aztecs.
- Cortes and his men had muskets, cross-bows and iron swords. The Aztecs had bows and arrows, and weapons made of wood and obsidian. So Cortes had better weapons than the Aztecs.
- The 'tribute' tribes fought with Cortes against the Aztecs. So the Aztecs had 300, 000 men. Cortes had 400 Spaniards, but hundreds of other Indians fought with him.
- Montezuma decided not to fight Cortes when they got to Tenochtitlan.
- The Aztecs began to fight back against Cortes. BUT Cortes killed the Aztec commanders so that there would be no-one to give orders. So Cortes was a clever leader. The Aztecs had no leaders left to help them.

9 What was life like in Spain?

Hernan Cortes had defeated the Aztecs. Their great city, Tenochtitlan, was in ruins. Their empire was no more. What would Cortes do now? Would he go back to Spain? Or would he try to build a new Spain in Mexico? Cortes had grown up in Spain at the time of King Ferdinand and Queen Isabella. What was it like to live in a Spanish town then?

Seville was a busy, wealthy town at the time of Ferdinand and Isabella. There were markets, shops and churches. There were houses for rich and poor people. Like most Spanish towns it had a large open square in the middle. Around the square were large houses and public buildings like the town hall. There were shops and small workshops on the roads which led from the square. A market was held in the main square. People went to the market to buy things like cloth, iron cooking pots, hens, geese, eggs, cheese, oil, wine and peaches. Unlike the Aztecs, Spanish people paid for these with money.

Nobles and rich merchants lived in houses with rooms which opened off a central courtyard. The floors were tiled. They sprinkled the tiles with water to keep the houses cool. Rich people had fine glass, silver candlesticks, carved wooden cupboards and chairs with soft cushions. Poor people lived in one roomed houses. Their floors were made of earth. They had wooden plates, pottery water jugs and a pile of rugs for a bed.

Source A

Hernan Cortes.

- The Aztecs did not use money for buying and selling. The Spanish did.
- Rich and poor Aztecs had different sorts of houses. They lived in different parts of Tenochtitlan.
- Rich and poor people in Seville lived in different sorts of houses. They lived in different parts of Seville.

A modern painting of the market in Seville.

At the beginning of the 1500s nearly everyone in western Europe was a **Christian**. All these Christians were Roman Catholics. In Spain the Catholic Church was very powerful and very rich. There was only one person richer than the Archbishop of Toledo, and that was King Ferdinand. The Catholic Church owned a lot of land. Bishops and archbishops built fortresses on Church lands and organised private armies. This was to make sure the Church kept its land and buildings safe from enemies.

Some people from North Africa, called **Moors**, lived in southern Spain. Most of the Moors were Muslims. There were a lot of **Jews** living in Spain. King Ferdinand and Queen Isabella wanted everybody to be Christian. Hundreds of Jews and Moors were forced to be **baptised** as Christians, although many of them carried on with their old religions in secret.

A group of churchmen in Spain had to make sure that everyone obeyed the teaching of the Catholic Church. They were called the **Inquisition**. People were not allowed to do or say anything against the Catholic Church. Sometimes people were accused of saying something against the Church. The Inquisition questioned them in a Church court. If they were found guilty, they were punished or even killed.

This wooden carving was made in Spain in 1520 by a man called Felipe Bigarny. It shows Moors being baptised. The carving is now part of an altar in Granada cathedral.

Pedro Berruguete painted this picture in 1500.
It shows what the Inquisition did to people.

Religion in Spain

- Most people in Western Europe at this time were Christians.
- All these Christians were Roman Catholics.
- The Catholic Church was very rich and powerful.
- There were people of other religions in Spain at this time. There were Jews and Moors. Moors were Muslims.
- The Spanish Inquisition tried to make sure that everyone obeyed the teaching of the Catholic Church. If they did not they were burned.

At the time of Ferdinand and Isabella children in Spain did not have to go to school. Children were taught what their parents thought they would need to know when they were grown up. The children of rich merchants and nobles were taught at home when they were young. They learned to read and write. The boys then went to schools run by the Catholic Church. They learned Latin, Greek and mathematics. Some of the schools were **choir schools**. In these schools the boys also learned to sing in church services. The girls stayed at home and learned singing, dancing, lute playing, sewing, painting and everything they would need to be a nobleman's wife.

The children of poor people learned to help their parents. They learned how to look after sheep, weave cloth, catch rabbits, plane wood, bake bread, sail ships and gut fish. These were skills they needed to have when they were grown up. The Catholic Church also ran schools for boys and girls whose parents were so poor they could not afford to look after them, or for children whose parents had died.

This is a page from a book made in Spain in about 1490. The picture shows a university teacher and his students. Only the sons of the very rich went to university.

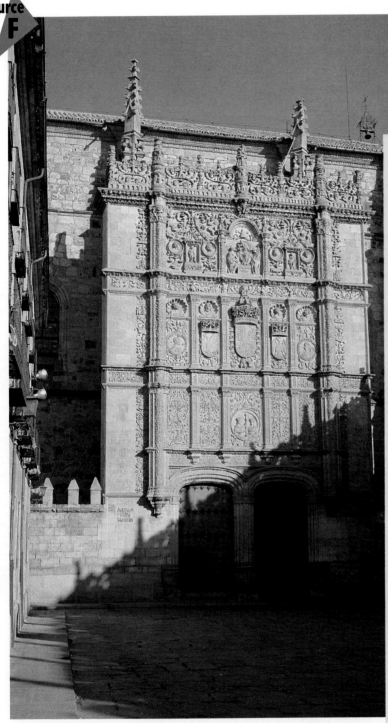

This is a modern photograph of part of the front of the university of Salamanca. All the stonework was finished in 1529. At the top is a carving of the Pope who was head of the Catholic Church. Can you find King Ferdinand and Queen Isabella?

How do we know?

We know about Spain in the early 16th century from many different types of sources.

- From pictures painted at the time, like Source A on page 48 and Source D on page 51.

- From carvings like the one in Source C on page 50.

- From books which we still have, like Source E on page 52.

- From buildings which still stand, like the one in Source F on page 53.

These sources show us that the Spanish were ...

... interested in learning.
... skilled stone-carvers.
... clever artists.
... skilled wood-carvers.

Why do we know more about Spain in the 15th and 16th centuries than we do about the Aztecs?

10 What happened to the Aztecs?

Source A

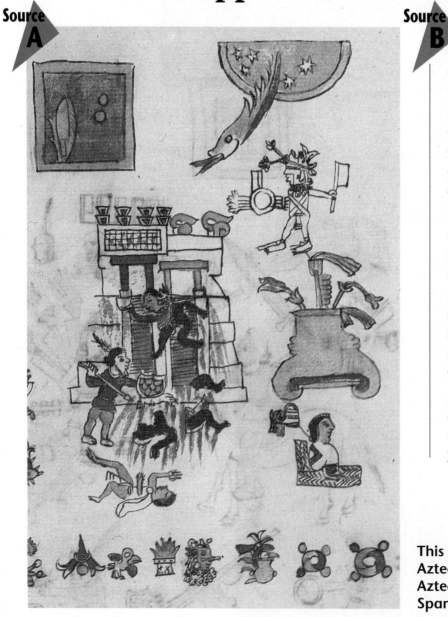

Source B

All three causeways were crowded with men, women and children so thin, dirty and stinking that it was pitiful to see them. Once the city was free from them Cortes went to inspect it. We found the houses full of corpses. The city looked as if it had been ploughed up. The roots of any plants had been dug out, boiled and eaten, and they had even cooked the bark of some of the trees. There was no fresh water to be found.

Bernal Diaz travelled with Cortes. He wrote this description many years later.

This picture was made by Aztecs in 1520. It shows Aztecs being killed by Spanish soldiers.

As soon as the last Aztec had left Tenochtitlan, Cortes and his men moved in. The Spaniards cleared the city. Anything still standing was pulled down. Soon there was nothing left of Tenochtitlan. Cortes and his men built Christian churches out of the stones of the Aztec temples. Then they built houses and shops. Gradually the Spaniards built a new, Spanish town where Tenochtitlan had been. They called the town **Mexico City**. It is still there today.

This picture was made in the 1500s. It shows Brother Domingo, a Spanish priest, teaching some Aztecs.

Aztec Empire becomes New Spain

- The Spanish pulled down Tenochtitlan. They built a Spanish city instead. Today this city is called Mexico City. It has a badge which you can see on page 23. This shows part of the story of the building of Tenochtitlan. It shows an eagle on a cactus with a snake. You can read this story on page 23.

- The Spanish tried to stop the Aztecs from worshipping their gods. They made them become Christians.

The Aztecs fled from Tenochtitlan to other villages and towns. The Spaniards stopped them, and all the other Indians living in Mexico, worshipping their gods. The Spaniards stopped them making sacrifices to their gods. They built churches all over Mexico and forced the Aztecs and other Indians to become Christians. Roman Catholic **missionaries** sailed from Spain to teach them all about Jesus Christ and his mother, Mary. Most Aztecs hoped the new Christian god would be better than their old ones, who had not protected them from the Spanish invaders. Many Aztecs were not happy about having just one god. The Spanish missionaries gave the Aztecs crucifixes and statues of the Virgin Mary. Most Aztecs just added them to their household gods which they had kept secretly.

The Catholic missionaries did not only teach the Aztecs about religion. They set up church schools and taught reading, writing and Spanish. The missionaries, and most people who lived in Europe, believed that there was only one right way to live and that was the European way. They believed that there was only one god, and that was the Christian God. The missionaries thought they were helping the Indians to live good lives.

Men and women came out from Spain and became farmers in Mexico. They brought horses and carts with them. The Aztecs learned how to use wheels and iron. The Aztecs and other Indians had to work for the Spanish. In return the Spanish were supposed to protect them and make sure that they became good Catholics. What actually happened was that the Spanish forced the Aztecs to work as their slaves.

King Charles I of Spain was the grandson of King Ferdinand and Queen Isabella. He did not want the Aztecs and other Indians to be treated badly. He tried to make things better, but Spain was a long way away and news and information travelled slowly. The people who went out to Mexico in the early days wanted to get rich quickly. They did not want to stay there for long. They wanted to make a fortune and get back to Spain. There they could live in luxury for the rest of their lives. They were determined to get as much work out of the Aztecs as they could.

This is part of a map of Mexico which was made by Alonso de Santa Cruz in 1550.

Thousands of Aztecs died during the fighting. Millions more died afterwards. Diseases like smallpox, measles and chicken-pox did not exist in Mexico before the Spanish arrived. When the Aztecs caught these diseases from the Spaniards, they became very ill indeed and many of them died.

Thousands of Aztecs died because of the way the Spanish settlers treated them. The Aztecs were not used to the kind of work the Spaniards expected them to do. They died from accidents, from overwork and from pneumonia.

Source E

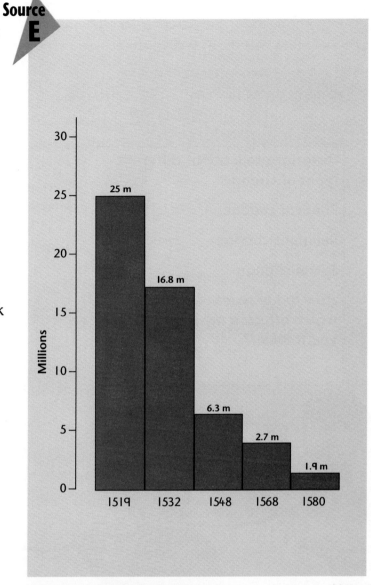

This bar-chart shows the number of Indians living in Mexico in the 1500s.

In August 1521 Tenochtitlan was destroyed. The Aztec empire was no more. Cortes now commanded all the lands which the Aztecs once ruled.

Charles I was now King of Spain. He was the grand-son of King Ferdinand and Queen Isabella. On October 15

1522 Cortes had a letter from King Charles. The letter told Cortes that he was now Governor and Captain-General of New Spain. Cortes built a new city where Tenochtitlan had been. The Spanish made the Aztecs into slaves.

How did things change?

Things changed for the Aztecs after Tenochtitlan was destroyed in 1521

- the Aztecs were no longer powerful rulers of an empire

> Historians talk about different types of change.
>
> **Political change**
>
> **Religious change**
>
> **Social change**
>
> *How many types of change which affected the Aztecs can you think of?*

- some Aztecs stayed and worked for the Spanish
- the Spanish took other Aztecs back to Spain as slaves
- the Spanish tried to make the Aztecs stop worshipping their gods
- the Spanish showed the Aztecs how to make and use iron BUT they took away their god and silver
- before 1519 25 million Aztecs lived in Mexico. By about 1550 there were only 6.3 million living there

Source F

The Spanish found out where the Aztec gold and silver mines were. They found out where the Aztecs' treasure houses were. They discovered where they made their jade jewellery, their feathered shields, their rich dyes, their cotton cloth and their chocolate. The Spaniards forced the Aztecs to hand over all the precious and wonderful things they had made. Everything had to go back to Spain. They forced the Aztecs to work for them as slaves down the gold and silver mines. Ships sailed for Spain, laden with treasure.

Source G

Learning from Montezuma's account books the names of the places which sent him tributes of gold, and where the mines and chocolate and cotton-cloths were to be found, we decided to go to these places.

Bernal Diaz, who travelled with Cortes, wrote this many years later.

This modern painting shows the Spanish in control of the Aztec slaves.

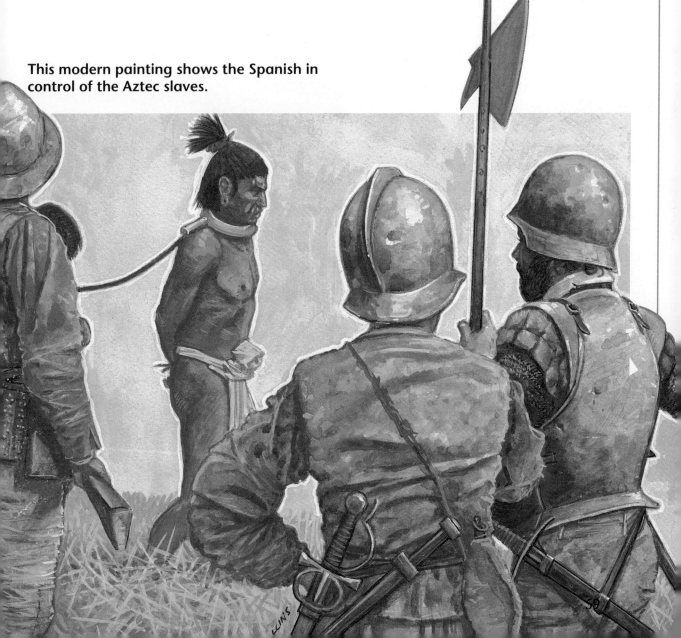

59

11 What happened to Spain?

Source A

The treasure from Mexico was taken up the **river Guadalquivir** to Seville. Seville was the only Spanish city which was allowed to trade with overseas lands which belonged to Spain. It was a rich and exciting port. The treasure ships unloaded gold, silver, jade and pearls. These were taken by carts to the royal warehouses. The royal warehouses were full of sugar, cocoa, leather and skins as well. Oil, wine, glass and fine silks were loaded on to ships. These sailed back across the Ocean Sea. These were for the Spanish people who had decided to settle in Mexico.

After about 1525 the markets in Seville sold more things than those you saw in the picture on page 49. They sold maize, tobacco, kidney beans, pineapples, sunflowers, tomatoes, peppers, avocado pears, chocolate, potatoes and marrows. They sold turkeys. All these new vegetables, fruits and animals were brought to Spain from America.

Spanish nobles, merchants and businessmen grew very rich. They made a lot of money selling goods to overseas lands which belonged to Spain. The gold, silver and pearls pouring in to the Spanish king's treasury made him very rich as well.

This is a picture of the docks at Seville, in Spain. It was painted in the early 1500s.

Information box

- In 1556 there was a new King of Spain. He was Philip II, the son of Charles I of Spain. King Philip II gave Seville a special licence to deal with all the trade which came from the New World.

- Seville became a very rich city. Thousands of people lived there. There were many beautiful buildings. King Philip had a huge palace built, called the Escorial (Source C on page 62). He built this with money from the riches brought in from America.

- The Spanish planted sugar cane in Central and South America. Sugar cane did not grow well in Spain. It needed a lot of hard work to grow sugar cane properly. The Spanish thought that the Aztecs would not work hard enough. They brought over slaves from Africa to work for them in America. They made a lot of money from selling sugar to Europeans.

- Later people from other European countries started to take slaves from Africa to work in America. Traders took tobacco and sugar from America to Europe and made a lot of money. This became known as the 'Triangular Trade'.

In 1560 Spain was the richest country in Europe. Spain owned more land overseas than any other European country. The Spanish empire in America stretched for thousands of kilometres, from north of Mexico to Peru. Spanish missionaries converted millions of Indians to Christianity. Spain was the most powerful country in the world.

From his palace in Madrid King Philip made sure that his empire was run properly. He set up a special council which sent officials to Mexico and Peru who made sure his orders were obeyed. The council told King Philip what his officials were doing.

Many Spanish people went out to live in Mexico and Peru. They set up cattle ranches, vineyards and sugar and banana plantations. They built fine houses. They took plants and crops from Europe. They sowed wheat, barley and rye; they planted apple, cherry, peach and plum trees; they grew herbs like rosemary and thyme. They took African slaves to work in the sugar and banana plantations.

Other countries in Europe began exploring the American continent. By 1650 merchants from England, France, the Netherlands and Portugal were trading with people in America. 160 years earlier most people in Europe didn't even know that America existed.

Source B

This picture was made in 1594. It shows Indians working in gold mines for the Spanish mine owners.

Source C

This picture was made in 1595. It shows Indians collecting pearls for Spanish traders.

What do people say about the past?

'The Aztecs were lucky. They were happy with their new lives.' — Pedro

'The Spanish taught the Aztecs to make iron. They gave them horses. They showed them how to use a wheel. The Aztecs had jobs. They worked in mines. They collected pearls.' — Ilsa

'The Aztecs did not do well. They were unhappy in their new lives. The Spanish were cruel to them.' — Rema

'The Aztecs became slaves. They had to speak Spanish. The Spanish destroyed Tenochtitlan. Thousands of Aztecs died from illnesses.' — Hank

'The Spanish taught the Aztecs to make iron. They gave them horses. They showed them how to use a wheel. The Aztecs had jobs. They worked in mines. They collected pearls.'

'The Aztecs were lucky. They were happy with happy with their new lives.'

'The Aztecs became slaves. They had to speak Spanish. The Spanish destroyed Tenochtitlan. Thousands of Aztecs died from illnesses.'

'The Aztecs did not do well. They were unhappy in their new lives. The Spanish were cruel to them.'

So why do different people say different things about the Aztecs?

INDEX